AGAINST EMPTINESS

Also by Paul Zweig

AGAINST EMPTINESS

Poems

by PAUL ZWEIG

HARPER & ROW, PUBLISHERS
NEW YORK, EVANSTON, SAN FRANCISCO, LONDON

1817

The following poems first appeared in these magazines:

Chelsea Review: "America at War"

Hudson Review: "Inside the Face," "The Bicycle Odyssey"

Kayak: "The Fate of Talking," "My Unfilled Spaces," "The Red Flower Poems," "Against Emptiness," "On Discovering a Thighbone"

The Nation: "Taking Off the Face," "Don't Walk," "On Willpower," "Looking Out at Night over Rooftops," "The Prayer Wheel," "Woman in a Window"

Poetry: "The Faces," "Walking over Brooklyn," "Gifts for the Silent Boy," "Listening to Gregorian Chant in San Marco, Venice," "The Marriage," "Voyage to Tasmania"

Poetry Bag: "Book of the Dead," "A Sadness from the Old Philosophers," "Survival," "The News"

The Sixties: "Night"

Sumac: "Wanted, Not Wanted," "Get the World into Your Poem," "Running," "Afraid That I Am Not a Poet"

University Review: "Self and Soul"

FIRST EDITION

LIBRARY OF CONGRESS CATALOG CARD NUMBER: 79-123974

for Francine

CONTENTS

Part One

ON DISCOVERING A THIGHBONE UNDER A HEAP OF STONES

I

I'm waiting for the Druid to claim his bone
In the woodshed. I have dusted and cleaned it,
But the stain of earth remains.
When he comes I will ask him to explain
These ancient stones heaped near the house
Like a ruined altar. Was he the priest
Who swore the earth to silence, or the victim
Whose blood sealed a pact with the spirit
Of revenge? I will ask him why the fields
Roar each night, as if they waited for
An answer; and tell him what cold secrets
I mumble in my fear, when the night air
Echoes them from tree to tree.

II

Spirits of the earth go by, like travelers
Along an empty road. Their bodies shake
Hungrily and their faces stare, but they
Refuse my hospitality. If one of them
Stumbles near me like a scoured bone,
I hold on to him angrily. What news, I ask.
But already my hands close on wet soil.
So it is each time I stop a traveler,
Until I too stumble in the dark field,
A pilgrim now, dying into earth
At every human touch.

THE FACES

Inside me I see faces,
Pushing hard against the light.

One fair-skinned, with pain etched in her voice,
And her body leaping on the canvas:
Angry shapes, shadows of the fear
She mends with cold, innocent color.

My grandmother bends over me
With fierce eyes, unhurried cheeks,
The years turn back inside her hands,
More fluent than voices.

And now my father's quiet face;
A flood of clear water sparkles near him.
I run my hands over the cold surface,
Unable to drink.

BOOK OF THE DEAD

Morning;
A still earthquake runs for miles
Through the streets;

Skyscrapers rise straight and stiff
Like the high crest of the iguana.

There is no place in my body for such days;
No place for this ring of leaky hearts
Wired for life,
These dolls scattered in the garden.

Fragments of myself come back,
The erratic, underwater people;
And I remember a sea robin with fleshy whiskers,
Eyes without lids,
Half-twisted, half-smeared over the deck;
A small monster, bristling and helpless.

My father stands over the spilled blood.
I cannot accuse him, as he
Motions me closer to the world's edge,
Until suddenly I remember;
I have been here before: this beach
With its charred grass,

Its smell of stranded fish.
I have been seduced before by the great
Talkers, exchanging their personal suffering
For a book written by the dead.

WALKING OVER BROOKLYN

Black smoke trails from the incinerators,
Bits of cardboard flaming in the cage
On top of tall chimneys.
You are walking over Brooklyn,
Climbing the space between planets.

Below you, the streets have a smell of childhood:
Rows of clotheslines, like an unsteady road
Where only ghosts can walk;
The murderous echo of boys playing
In the damp shadow of tenements.

You can hear them climbing toward you,
Listen! pulling you down
Like a weathered kite, hand over hand.

At the dinner table, old people sit,
Their bodies locked in the shell
Of the long days; in their eyes,
Dim corridors lit by candles,
Like the pure distance I once tasted
In my blood.

You gave me what I didn't want
And taught me to love it. You fed me
Sweet food, and killed each painful cell
To read the bitter news I stored there:
News of the smile I crammed against my teeth,
Until angels danced on my nerves
And the gates of heaven opened in my eyelids.

I swear to love what you will take away,
I swear that my bones will be a signature
To bind me in all the courts of heaven:

Owed, my body and the death that cures it.
Owed, these torn pockets to collect your charity.
My aim: to lose more than you give,
Lying down in the hole I have made,
Window upon which death leans,
Me.

A SADNESS FROM
THE OLD PHILOSOPHERS

I plant my stick in the loose earth,
And now my father lies down beside me.

I mean the old philosophers,
Emerson, Thoreau,
Mirrors broken, put back together
In silence;

And Walt Whitman,
Grazing at the edges of the earth,
Becoming grass.

WOMAN IN A WINDOW

My mother sleeps in the cradle of her hands,
Her son gallops inside her like a cloud.

≈

She walks in the empty lot near the house,
Between blocks of ruined concrete,
Remembering voices
Bleached by long exposure.

≈

In this canyon, heat flows over the rocks.
Fish lie wrapped in shadow,
Motionless, made of red ochre;
Fish old as the morning, their harsh
Sand-mouths flattened against the rock.

ON POSSESSIONS

Burning what I own,
Burning this fuel of nerves and money;

Soon I will be a voice hidden among ruins,
Too poor to be flesh.

The fire climbs in my lush veins,
Gutting the landscape,
Destroying my fresh gardens
With flowers rejoicing as they burn,
To mourn for me with ashes still warm:
They are new clothing for the skeleton voyager
Who travels where he cannot see,
Letting the emptiness play him like a harp;
His music heard only by the poor
Who play it upon their bones.

Did the saints know this, leaping
In the fire, snapping their fingers?
Their bodies hummed quarter tones and half tones;
And the dumbest trooper shrank into his skin,
Knowing that he could reach no further
With his glowing iron; that a god
Smiled in this wound,
And crawled in this burning flesh.

Earth, edible darkness,
Reminding me that I am a plant
Without roots, and that's all.
For my mobility I pay with hunger;
And the wind knows what to do with me,
Raging in my throat like a judgment,
Spending my poor substance, year by year,
Until I am the wind, resolved into
Its movement, settling finally
In a field where food awaits me,
And no wind.

AFRAID THAT I AM NOT A POET

Afraid that I am not a poet,
Yet willing to write
Even about that;
Holding up words I have loved,
Their exploded joys
Have scarred me into life,

And I am frightened suddenly.
For nothing I have been resembles them;
Nothing has stuck to these
Irretrievable bones.

How can I be sane with borrowed faces?
When the fears and pleasures
That tumble my words
Like seasons harvested in love,
Are only empty mirrors,
Images floating in a dry sea?

THE NATURAL HISTORY OF DEATH

I

I decided at birth to go on living,
Not even my parents convinced me I was wrong.
When the mistake was pointed out
I excused myself,
Alleging my extreme youth.

I liked standing naked in the basement
Shoveling coal into the open furnace.
The heat taught me I had a body
Long before women ever tried.
That is why, even now, love begins for me
In madness, as if this were an answer
To the old question:
What have you done to need life so badly?

II

When they pried open my life
They found
Mechanical toys and a taste for pure light;

They heard a voice calling backward
In the fibers of the body.

I went out late at night, with poems
Rolled under my arm, pasting them
On storefronts and parked cars;
Talking to the desperate faces:
To skeletons softened by light,
And those who were in no hurry to live.

When they pried open my life
They found
A memory twisted as old iron,
Ice-age fingers innocent as murder.

III

Somewhere in my body a cell must still remember
The flower-smells, the carriage floating
Along the paths of the Botanical Gardens
In Brooklyn.

Columns of black smoke slanted over Europe,
Stepladders
For the meek bodies of the burned.

IV

Who felt with me for the delicate bones
Emerging from boyhood?

Still hungry, and with a man's thoughts,
I ransacked the quiet rooms.
Empty, the world was served up to me,
Like derelict children, piling up
Minute by minute.
They stiffened, and I pressed them
In an old book, before they lost their color.

V

Like mirrors, my hands
Held only what was put into them.
Scraps of paper drowned near the curb
In the rushing water, bearing
My possessions, one by one:
My love for words;
Glasses filled with wax, flickering
For the dead,
Praying for me out of my mother's fear,
And her mother's wild thoughts
In Poland,
Dreaming of the Revolution.

VI

Later, guns learned to resist us,
Firing salvos of raw meat;
The sweet smile of men unwilling to live
Set fire to their houses.

We were sleepy old men, coming of age;
Silent men,
Far in advance of the dictionary.

But the quiet people would not grow up;
They practiced making love under their beds,
They practiced living forever.

Where is the terror that rots under the shirt front?
Where is the child who climbed
On the back of a dog, and crossed America? . . .

VII

At thirty, a man discovers that he has told
A secret. His eyes whisper, while the shouting
In his head goes on, too quick to understand.

The wasted minutes hang
Like a halo of lines around his face.

Words become human as they sink out of reach,
Already bored with being said,
But sweaty,
Expectant. His words listen to themselves,
Like an eye gradually closing,
Making the body-ruins transparent,
But who is there to be seen?

Part Two

THE FATE OF TALKING

There has been enough hysteria.
Instead of biting life we bite ourselves.
Our rivers have run together like navigable sleep,
And the danger loiters without innocence.

Should we meet the dark lady in our skulls,
We do not kill ourselves outright; having
Acquired the skill of talk, we explain
To her our personal destruction.

But now nothing can scare us into dreaming;
Our nights are like stones, our days
The letters chipped into them: "Here lies . . ."
To finish the inscription
You must destroy the stone.

Affairs are worsening in the city of bare fact.
Cars, racing past all the exits,
Collapse of decency and hunger.

Night sticks whisper to the broken heads . . .

These children who dream with open eyes,
These children protect us. Their stringy music
Wanders in the brain, to come out
In later years, a story pieced together
By old age, the one secure misery.

TODAY I WILL ADMIRE

Today I will admire the miracle of my body,
That it should know enough to stay alive,
Uninfluenced by the example set for it
In the street, where people are helping
Each other to bullets and strong opinions,
And when you feel something warm,
It is not love, but blood.

He lies under the broad leaves,
Waiting for soldiers
To walk noisily behind the hill,
And bodies of the dead to gather
Silence over them.

∽∾

The hunter leans against a birch tree
In the yellow afternoon.
His boots scar the moss-covered stones;
The quietness, sucked like a breath
Out of the broken-chested bird
At his feet.

∽∾

I discovered these faces in the dirt,
And played with them, asking them
Questions, unable to pull the faces
Off, because they fit.

ON WILLPOWER

Ambush in peace,
You will destroy the shadow
That lies in ambush around you.

Only the animal
You are not hunting will be seen,
Although leaves shake with concealed life;

Only the unbaited hook
Is sweet for fish.

The shaken branch hungers
For its own fruit.

WANTED, NOT WANTED

I dream of killing you,
Searching in my hands
For the muscle that will express you,
The nerve aimed at your life
Like impersonal laughter.

But when my dream grows heavy,
Like the small enjoyment
Of which we are no longer capable,
Who will instruct my grief?

DON'T WALK

It said don't walk,
I didn't walk.
It said lie down,
I opened my book, answering it:
"On my rights as a citizen of this book
I will not lie down; I will walk.
At the bloody games I will shout for blood,
Leaving my mother out of it,
Rubbing my eyes for sheer wonderment.
I will not confess that I am a man."

Images arise in me, in pairs;
Yesterday they brought me a lump of fat
With wrinkles I could read:
DON'T WALK,
I didn't walk.
LIE DOWN,
And I opened my book.

I

I work at night, carried
By conveyor belts from one sex to another,
Tired of being loved.

When I kill, it is complicated,
Instantaneous.
I crouch inside the gun,
Waiting for the detonation, fondling
Letters from home.
In a moment I will spring,
Knowing
That technology cannot replace me.

II

How can I escape the invisible father and mother?
Their obedient anger
Reaping swaths of broken trees
In the green wood?

My longing cannot be silenced,
It quivers in these cold buildings.

III

Even the elephants know us,
As they wallow in gasoline fumes,
Refusing to make love,
The rivers of elephant pleasure
Corked up in their great legs.

SURVIVAL

You must work at your body,
Old bones are not measured in radium.

Those footprints springing behind you
Return to dust
As you head for death-country.

∽∾∽

To survive,
To invent a grave for my confused thoughts.

We stand around in the afterworld
Saluting ghosts, longing for pain,
But our own pain, recognizable.
That is what we lost when we died.

I will name nature's poisons.

Chiendent, the spread of its roots
Like a slum of hungry mouths.

Mushroom, nourishing danger,
Sweated by feverish oaks and chestnuts,
Their delectable cancer.

Angular rocks, scales of the great leprosy,
Torn by God's wheel of changes
Working its wound into the earth.

Viper, threading the grass
With its charge of perfect electricity.
Beetles designed by Picasso to be African gods.
Lizards so harmless I lie awake
Imagining their secret weapon.

These are my companions in your green plague,
Virgin of sweet rot. In my anguish
I match you poison for poison, and fight off
Your blandishing quiet. I dine upon
A soup of nerves and bask in the human,
My body bent into a sign against your
Treachery of flowers.

Part Three

AGAINST EMPTINESS

I

Whatever surrounds the raw body of wind
And rolls over me in silence;
Whatever I am this screaming silence for . . .

I want to climb to you, foot by foot,
Along the prayer ladder:
Dusky flower,
Gloom tree in the nerves,
And then my body rigged with magic,
Crying to fill that great invention, your emptiness,
Your tricky silences between stars.

II

The prophet casts his life upon the water;
Upon the waking fish and those, asleep,
Who interpret their solitude without end.
They ascend by their teeth,
By the cell rot of unaccomplished days,
Each small death tidied into words, until
The walls of dead enclose them, and they are
Grateful to be remembered by their failures.

III

Know these words: demon, angel,
And they will follow as you climb
From pit to pit, leaving behind each day
A cell of your rage, a life,
Until, exhausted into wisdom,

Your face will ease you into death;
Your wise face, shedding its peacefulness
Like a lie upon your angry children,
Your patient devils, and the intricate
Joy of the angels you never named.

MEDITATIONS

Branches creak upright against the rain,
Dropping bitter nuts, harsh
Burry skins, mysterious to smell.

❧

Look, flowers common as air,
Ignorant petals,
Too powerful in their delicate flesh;
Worth only the pleasure of a glance,
Like a child distracted by so much beauty.

❧

The cold heart beats quietly,
And I stutter, imitating as best I can
Its prayer:
        heart-song of wood,
Small memories worn into a human shape
By so much need.

Words I couldn't say turned to anger
And sank into my face;
Seeds in the dried earth,
Blinded by sunlight.

A face is destroyed
By the words it has forgotten.

The yellow flower
Never leaves its well in the root;
Never takes its place
On the clear plain of the cheeks,
Over the eyes,
In the shadowy strength of the chin.

MUSHROOM HUNTING

Cold meat, tempting me deeper and deeper
In the woods, drawn not by hunger
But by loneliness; touching these curious
Domes to find what doors may open
In the rotted floor. I crawl over spongy leaves,
And pick handfuls of death-meat,
Its cool eyes staring into me
In the crazy quiet of the chestnuts;
Until the forest draws its curtain
All around me, and I climb into the earth,
Trying to reach my body climbing under me,
Bearing me like a shadow over the gentle cauldron,
These mushrooms, its odorous bubbles.

I note down this progress: a night survived,
An hour's truce with that sweet surprise,
My life, of which today I will ask so little.
Maybe, now, someone remembers me somewhere,
But when the wind hurries by me on the hillside
As if it had somewhere to go,
I am thankful to be left behind.

MY UNFILLED SPACES

I embark at night; water
Hissing under the keel
Like dry leaves.

My oars encounter no resistance,
And I am free to have all the emotions.

Behind the earth, looking down, I see
The unfilled spaces; an explosion
Of white stars, heaving
With light like grave-flowers.
I follow them
Through all the connecting spaces,
Leaving myself forever.

❧

Weeds prod my skin, and I think
Which desert I will cross:
The grey angular one sloping
To home, or this quiet one
I discover when the world will not
Remind me of myself.

LOOKING OUT AT NIGHT
OVER ROOFTOPS

I

Voices ride in from the horizon,
Pale bears tumbling end over end,
Hair in their eyes, blotting out the stars,
Leaving a musty odor in the night, like rain.

II

Which of these lights is my own,
Which has been carried by the darkness
That falls in my sleep?

III

Shipwreck! The ribs of the boat spreading
Like petals; columns of grey water
Lift up and dissolve. Trees
With foaming roots; desperate thoughts.

GIFTS FOR THE SILENT BOY

I

Lost in my skin all day, a bird,
Its small cries troubling the afternoon,
As if nothing were near but miles
Of scrub pine, a horizon of white hills
Needing water.

II

My mother sits in a room, at her side
Baskets with towels over them:
Gifts for the silent boy.

III

Rocks lay in the water, the sun leaping
From their surface like small fires.
I laughed. I had forgotten something.
I was entirely alone.

IV

Sitting in a distant city, I see faces
Like sparks falling into a calm sea.
I am ready now. The earth
Slips by me like the mooring
Of a huge balloon.

Let water lie flat between the trees
And wind blow toward us
From a place behind the sun.
Let my eyes see without holding on.

My sadness grows a body,
It hurries eastward over crowded roads,
Collapsing near me like a lost wheel.

PRIVATE REPORT

Shedding the blood of our nerves,
We learn to distrust ordinary things.

We are outdone by small creatures
Who leave their small mark in the snow:
Mice, grave rabbits, fools of the earth
Trailing their maps behind them
As they follow their needs into the necessary world.

THE DAY OF LILIES

I

When Pope John blessed the poor, quarries
Of earth-old pain arose to be blessed.
Skeletons climbed from their tombs
And the air became sweet with new bodies.
But the Pope, who could bless, could not
Speak with stones.

II

Condemned to its daily wound, the earth
Survived in hope, waiting for the Day of Lilies,
Jakob Boehme's day, when the living
Would take root like angry flowers
Pleading through cracks in their skin.

III

Water rises in the earth, like pools
Of the ancient blood, and a great hope
Flings past me:
                  whisper of oracles
On a dry roof; all the groping languages
I hear now in my summer of waiting and listening.

TWO POEMS ABOUT ANGELS

Angels are grazing in the spring grass.
Their light flows upward,
And the sun drains it away.

⁂

Behind me flowers spring erect,
Offering me the gift of weightlessness,
Gift of angels and spiders.

LISTENING TO GREGORIAN CHANT
IN SAN MARCO, VENICE

The martyrs come back
Loaded with ashes, rough stones,
Their prayers whispered like a low flame.

But the old saints are nailed to the wall;
Their voices drift along cold roads,
Side by side,
Like streaks of dim light.

NIGHT

It has depths fishermen still look for
And the strongest wind cannot enter;

Depths like rivers choked by weeds
And foul-smelling grass.

It has a man walking backward down a road,
Dressed like a child.

You sit near an old wreck, glowing eels
Circling in the water next to you.

Or are you that pilgrim up ahead, hurrying,
Led by a frightened old man?

I touched your shadow on the table,
Dreaming of luminous nebulae, those milky sisters,
And a vague stroll across the archipelagos.
That was our innocence.

Everything we touched was changed into our lives.
Husks of light fell between us,
Flowers too hard to pick;

And the trees resembled us. Their leaves
Touched with delicate, solitary movements,
Leaving behind the trunk with its harsh wood,
The cramped angle of branches leaping
Into space.

The trees: ships rooted in wind,
Unable to slip the deep anchors
That nourish and bind them.

VOYAGE TO TASMANIA

I

Trees listen!
Roads hurry on their knees
Past cities of red grass,
And animals waiting to be born.

The kings of Tasmania sleep in a stone.
They pull themselves awake by the roots of the earth.
Hang on, we are waking up, they cry!

II

I pass herds of the humped metaphor.
Its hair rubbed loose by old age
And one leg wrapped around its body,
It rolls downhill, stuccoed
With cities, trees, loose stones.
Study the humped metaphor,
Its life is written on its back!

III

Here is Walt Whitman, hanging from a tree.
He looks for days at the ground, loving himself.
Walt, I cry, Tasmania!
His hands clench and unclench
Like a slow wind. He talks,
Wild anemones spread their color on his knees,
Between his legs. Speak English, I yell!
Tasmania? The flowers point in all directions.

Growing old, I cannot lose my way.
In my pocket a letter for Tasmania
And a mirror to charm the weather.

Tasmania? I ask the great sloth,
But his breath tears me loose like bark
From an old tree. Get lost, he murmurs,
Empty your life. I dig holes
In the ground and bury my voice.
I take off my clothes and climb in after it.

V

The great sloth falls from his branch,
Floating all day like a hairy leaf,
And as he falls he sings to me:

—Seven crows went up the hill,
Their feathers naked to the quill.
They walked around inside their bones
Like apricots without their stones.

The awful pleasures of the air
Were far too much for them to bear.
They held their bones above their heads
And dreamed that they were feather beds.

Seven crows went down the hill,
Their bodies were invisible.
The air was filled with polka dots
Like stones without their apricots.

VI

My rivers become sand; my roads
Dissolve and turn to rain.

I lie down in the moving earth of the stream,
Letting go, turning over in the current
Like a bent stick. I will not reach the sea.
The earth clings to me like a flimsy cloud.
I dissolve in the lacy current,
Unable to feel pain.
The slowly rising air carries me to seed.

Part Four

THE RED FLOWER POEMS

I

I took some nails and knocked them
In the air. They gleamed and sparkled.
I ran my hands over the smooth walls
And laid down carpets for my feet. The room
I built myself from planks, nails, windows,
And lived in it.

Outside the trees sputtered
With cool, joyous flame;
Again people walked above ground.
Life came to me like a signal on the radio,
A mellow static pouring into the room between words.

"Weather report: sunlight and burning trees,
Red flowers and children." I lay down
On the floor, hearing these words
I loved, afraid of the weather.

II

A flower shot through the head
Comes to life again, despite
Our principles. When we talk,
I know I am looking for you.

III

The flower slips underground,
Losing its petals; it is
Going through a new phase,
As it prepares to meet the dead.

"We who have worn out our bodies
With our luck,
Getting rid of ourselves
Piece by piece,
As we practice keeping still;
We have absolutely no opinions."

The flower takes root among the dead,
Running amok
In a fog of petals, opinionated,
Outrageous,
Until the bones, bewildered,
Remember everything,
Unable to be dead any longer
In the old way.

A hand letting go,
A wish compressed until
It breaks apart,
The flower gives itself away.

GET THE WORLD INTO YOUR POEM

Get the world into your poem,
They tell me, as I try to explain
My confusion. What world do you mean,
I ask, and when they don't answer
I become frantic.

Forgetting the name of what I felt,
I leaned over the table, thinking:
Helpful table, scarred with use
And a desire to resemble the world!

Suspended at the falling-off point,
My feet dangling in the abyss,
I wonder how to get this table
Into the poem. My strategy:
To operate and crawl in after it.
I do this,
Buried in the silence like a line of poetry
That goes "this way."

The dwarf tears at his clothes
To greet the quietness.
He nudges me to show him what I write,
Although he knows all about my longing.
If I'm not careful, he'll
Tear the page and wipe himself with it.

When he falls under a chair, cooing
Like a baby, I will overcome
My native cowardice and trample him.
He will beg me to stop, but I'll
Soak him in whiskey and light a match
To it—by the flickering glare
Lying down with a book, to read:
Poetry, I think, about quietness
And corn growing, waking up somewhere
Too happy to wake up.

I have made my peace with the monster.
I will give him what I have,
In return he will give me nothing,
But I don't complain, for he
Is nervous and will drink himself mad
Before long.

Each night I dream of killing him,
But he knows the art of guilt.
He sleeps when I sleep, when
I eat, the food enters his mouth.
Making love, he lies down for me,

And he knows my ignorance:
The fear that when he lives for me,
I have no life: it is the fear
Eating and waking up, the noise
Of the body taking my place.

Tired now, he has fallen asleep.
And I remember what it is like
To have lost the power of movement;
To live only vertically;
To become a tree.

Running, sleeping on the run;
Yesterday
On paths of white dust, in quiet,
Running, men stooped over
The fingers of wheat,
Stating their case in rags,
Seamed cheeks,
Their legs rickety and crooked.
Dried wheat chatters in the wind,
Running,
Past holes in the road where huge drops
Of rain fell.

And now the next town, with its
Black chimney tops,
An ocean made of spilt conversation,
Running.

I get married on soft grass
Disturbing the linnets,
The bees and the common horsefly
With my naked body;
Running, holding her with forbidden hands,
Her body changing, her face changing,
But hold on, don't let go,
Running, sweating on the run.
The eternal woman comes to rest;
I will answer you, she says,
Smiling and running.

THE BICYCLE ODYSSEY

I

Sleep is no death, no familiar ordeal.
I will get up now and shape my body hopefully;
I will barricade this wild skin that brings its messages
To me past sleeping lions and monkeys,
And a chandelier of bones that sheds its light
Inside my body.

I will leave the small, mobile prisons:
My home where the space under the walls
Has been hollowed out by fear;
Streets rubbed smooth by the moon,
Like pale sandpaper humming over the curb
And the parked cars, and the stiff sex of the streetlights.

II

My wife looks out at me from the parked cars
And bangs at the windshield; she turns on
The radio, listening for news of the spirit.
There is my father, squatting on a leaf
High over the sidewalk. He follows the gentle
Footprints of a searchlight across the stars.
It is looking for a thin crack in the sky,
Leading to a place inside his thoughts
Which he has never loved.

He sits in the highest branches of the tree
As if he were enclosed in his name,
Waiting for me to wake up and return him to his body.

III

But I leaped on my old bicycle and hurried to the beach.
Sleep is a diving bell, a portable adventure.
The water curled aside and lisped.
It spread rugs of seaweed over my sleeping madness
And down I went, pedaling on the back of an eel.
As I went, my shirt fell off, and my pants;
Last of all I lost my straw hat.

IV

At the bottom of the sea I found a wrecked ship,
Its ribs twisted out of shape,
Its crew lifting and falling with the current
Like a field of lilies
Waiting to be resurrected. Strangest of all
Were its green sails that strained with the tide,
Glowing and stiff, a clear foliage of canvas.
I recognized the crew and called them by their names.
"Flowerpod," I called, "Skyscraper, Naked Bottle!"
"Words, words," they gurgled back at me,
"They sink in water and don't taste very good."

V

And then the lilies began to sing:

> A stovepipe hat
> and a motor car
> flew round and round
> the morning star.
>
> A flatiron
> straightened out the sky,

until the star
began to cry.

Then something
in a trolley car
tugged the sky
around the star.

Round and round
the star they went,
until the very sky
was bent.

Sink the sea
and go to shore;
your love don't love you
any more.

Their singing swam around me. It nibbled at my chest
And plucked my hair, and almost woke me up;
Until I rode away and put my sleep to sleep.

VI

I was naked, for my mind had fallen open.
But the lilies bowed and scraped;
They waved their boneless arms and saw,
As in an old movie, the bicycle,
The skinny legs, the awkward greeting
Of this man who had not known them.

VII

I saw an old man
With strands of seaweed between his legs,
Bright fish where his eyes had been.
He counted the days on a rosary of glowing stones.

Now and then he picked a day from the string,
Rough, angular, fiery, and ate it;
Tears rolled from his cheeks onto the ocean floor,
Where they lay, hardened by salt and cold,
Until this man, this father of all days,
Slipped one hand,
Beaked and marvelous like a cuttlefish,
Onto the pile of the days.

VIII

Then my bicycle rusted and I had to swim.
My skin fell off and I had to walk.
My legs melted and stretched,
My eyes wandered on a green thread
That I could lengthen or pull in, like radar.

I saw a woman buried in the sand;
She wore the ocean like a body.
Mother! I cried, crawling with eight strong arms
Over the sand.

IX

The wild, thinking water I had become
Arranged itself in ranks,
A transparent army, rushing through the fields
Of water, undiluted, tickled by long
Fingers of the moon.

Striped, spiney fish played inside me.
Electric eels plugged into me,
Sputtering messages. The whole ocean
Was resurrected by the currents
Of my intelligent, salty body.

Format by C. Linda Dingler
Set in Intertype Baskerville
Composed and printed by York Composition Company, Inc.
Bound by The Haddon Craftsmen, Inc.
HARPER & ROW, PUBLISHERS, INCORPORATED